Sound Phonics

Teacher's Resource Book

Carol Matchett

Schofield & Sims

Further resources are available as free downloads from the Schofield & Sims website (www.schofieldandsims.co.uk). These materials are updated as necessary to meet the requirements of the National Curriculum.

First published in 2014

Copyright © Schofield & Sims Limited 2014

Author: Carol Matchett
Carol Matchett has asserted her moral right under the Copyright, Designs and Patents Act, 1988, to be identified as the author of this work.

British Library Catalogue in Publication Data:
A catalogue record for this book is available from the British Library.

Commissioning by Carolyn Richardson Publishing Services (www.publiserve.co.uk)
Design by Oxford Designers & Illustrators
Printed in the UK by Wyndeham Gait Ltd, Grimsby, Lincolnshire

ISBN 978 07217 1224 6

Contents

Introduction

General resources — Tog posting box ● Voting paddles ● Phoneme frames ● Word sort sheets ● Phonic family tree ● Caption book ● Tricky word bookmarks ● Blank word cards

Activity book resources

Sound Phonics Phase One — Picture cards

Sound Phonics Phase Two — Phase Two and Three sound mat ● Tricky word mat one ● Stepping stones game ● Grapheme cards ● Phoneme frame letters ● Sound button words ● Reading sentences

Sound Phonics Phase Three — Phase Three sound mat ● Star blazer game ● Beanstalk game ● Against the clock

Sound Phonics Phase Three Book 1 — Grapheme cards ● Phoneme frame letters ● Sound button words ● Word cards ● Reading sentences

Sound Phonics Phase Three Book 2 — Grapheme cards ● Phoneme frame letters ● Sound button words ● Word cards ● Reading sentences ● Word cards: two-part words

Sound Phonics Phase Four — Word cards: two-part words ● Tricky word mat two ● Chimney game ● Phoneme frame letters ● Sound button words ● Word cards ● Reading sentences

Sound Phonics Phase Five — Phase Five sound mat ● Tricky word mat three ● Treasure trail game ● Maze game

Sound Phonics Phase Five Book 1 — Grapheme cards ● Phoneme frame letters ● Word cards ● Reading sentences ● Writing sentences ● Word cards: two-part words

Sound Phonics Phase Five Book 2 — Word cards: two-part words ● Word cards ● Reading sentences ● Story sentences ● Writing sentences

Sound Phonics Phase Five Book 3 — Word cards ● Phoneme spotting sentences ● Sentence starters

Sound Phonics Phase Six Book 1 — Word cards ● Introducing spelling guidelines ● Writing sentences

Sound Phonics Phase Six Book 2 — Word cards ● Learning to spell sentences ● Introducing proofreading ● Introducing prefixes and suffixes

Assessment resources — Phase One ● Phase Two ● Phase Three ● Phase Four ● Phase Five ● Phase Six ● Group letter formation record sheet

Introduction

Sound Phonics

Sound Phonics supports the teaching and learning of phonics. It builds knowledge systematically, moving incrementally from simple to more complex aspects of phonics work, developing the skills and knowledge needed to read and spell words.

The series follows the same basic structure as the phonics resource *Letters and Sounds* (© Crown copyright 2007) and includes the following components.

- The **Teacher's Guide** helps you, the teacher, parent or other adult helper, to teach phonics. It provides guidance on introducing key skills and knowledge, using the activity books and consolidating learning. Opportunities for the children to practise phonic skills and apply phonic knowledge are suggested.

- This **Teacher's Resource Book** contains photocopiable resources for use in the activities outlined in the **Teacher's Guide**. **General resources** are suitable for several Phases, while **Activity book resources** relate to specific books.

- **Rhymes for Reading** is a photocopiable collection of phonically decodable rhymes with accompanying **Teaching notes**, aimed at Phases Two to Four. These provide a valuable opportunity to apply phonic knowledge in a real reading context at an early level.

- The **activity books** are carefully graded and contain exercises to practise the phonic knowledge and skills introduced through teaching. The first book is a reusable stimulus book, while the remaining nine are one-per-child activity books. Clear teaching objectives are summarised at the foot of each page.

Note: the activity books, resource book and photocopiable rhymes may also be used to support other incremental phonics programmes.

Using Sound Phonics

Sound Phonics is based on the model 'teach → practise → apply → assess', as described below.

Teach

The **Teaching notes** in the **Teacher's Guide** explain how each learning focus can be introduced to a group or class of children, using interactive and multi-sensory activities. The learning focus is kept clear in short, direct sessions and this Resource Book provides materials to use in the activities.

Practise

The **Sound Phonics** activity books provide plenty of practice material to consolidate new learning. The activities are most effective if completed in a small group with an adult present, as this allows the children to make and listen to sounds, and to practise their phonic skills orally. Further practice activities are described in the **Teacher's Guide** and supported by material in this Resource Book.

Apply

From **Sound Phonics Phase Two**, the activity book exercises require the children to apply their phonic knowledge and skills to read decodable captions, sentences and questions, moving towards complete texts in Phase Six. In addition, this Resource Book contains word swap activities and sentences for reading and writing practice.

Rhymes for Reading provides phonically decodable rhymes for Phases Two to Four. These allow the children to apply their new phonic knowledge in a real reading context at an early stage.

The **Teacher's Guide** features 'Applying phonics' boxes, which recommend ways to apply phonic knowledge and skills in other areas of learning.

Assess

Each page in the activity books has a clear teaching objective, summarised in the 'Focus' notes, which helps to guide on-going assessment, and assessment tasks and statements are also included. Record and analysis sheets are provided in this Resource Book, and full details on carrying out assessments, analysing results and using the record sheets are given in the **Teacher's Guide**.

Sound Phonics Teacher's Resource Book

The **Sound Phonics Teacher's Resource Book** provides a bank of photocopiable resources to support the activities and assessments described in the **Teacher's Guide**.

Resources may be photocopied for individual and pair activities or enlarged onto A3 paper for group work. It may be appropriate to laminate and reuse some resources, while others can be used in class, then sent home for further practice.

The **Sound Phonics Teacher's Resource Book** includes:

● resources to support the introduction of a new focus

● materials for extension and reinforcement activities

● games to be used in the classroom or at home for extra practice

● analysis and record sheets for assessment tasks.

The resources are organised into the following sections.

General resources

These resources can be modified and used in different ways across several phases. They include phoneme frames and word sort sheets, as well as *voting paddles* and a *caption book* template. The *Tog posting box* can be used for sorting and learning activities throughout the series, while the *Phonic family tree* helps children to organise their new knowledge in an accessible form.

Activity book resources

These are aligned with specific pages in each activity book and can be used to introduce a new learning focus or support practice activities. Word cards and sentences feature known graphemes and tricky words appropriate to each activity book. Sound mats and tricky word mats help the children to recall graphemes and words in different contexts, and simple games provide fun opportunities for reinforcement without unnecessary distractions. Sentences with *words to swap* provide reading practice and familiarise the children with basic sentence structure.

Assessment resources

The record and analysis sheets are designed to accompany the assessment tasks found at the back of the activity books. You will find full details of how to carry out the assessments and how to use these sheets on pages 87–90 of the **Teacher's Guide**.

Stick the template onto a cereal box and cut out the mouth, so that the children can 'post' word and grapheme cards through. The **Tog posting box** can also be used in a range of blending and segmenting activities, as described in the **Teacher's Guide**.

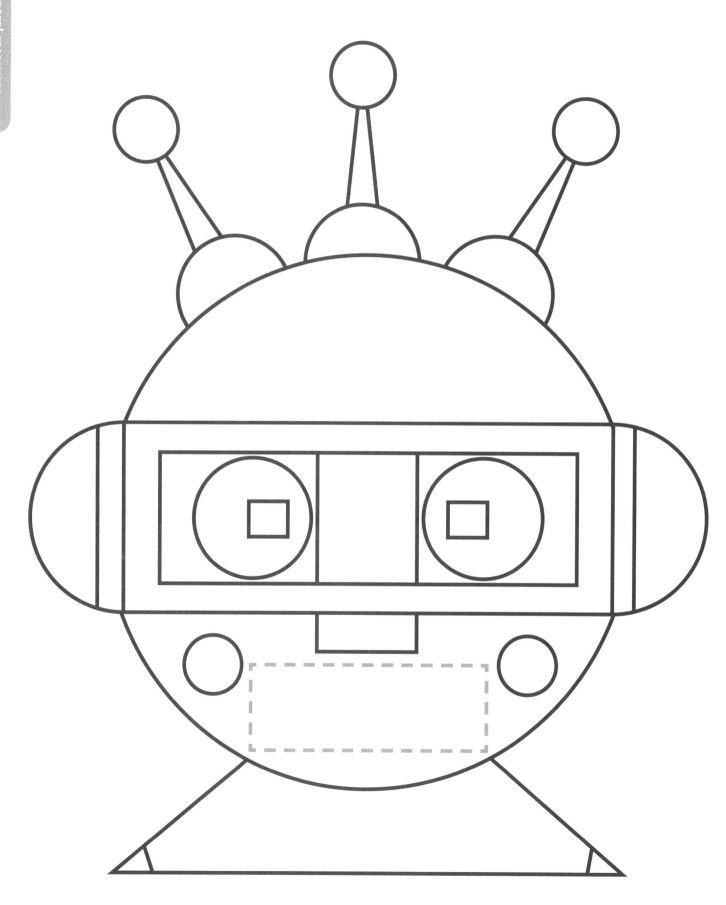

From: **Sound Phonics: Teacher's Resource Book** by Carol Matchett (ISBN 978 07217 1224 6). Copyright © Schofield & Sims Ltd, 2014. Published by Schofield & Sims Ltd, Dogley Mill, Fenay Bridge, Huddersfield HD8 0NQ, UK (www.schofieldandsims.co.uk). This page may be photocopied after purchase for use within your school or institution only.

Stick paddles onto card and give to the children to indicate their answers, for example, make yes and no *paddles* or **ee** and **ea** *paddles. The children should then hold up the paddles to answer questions.*

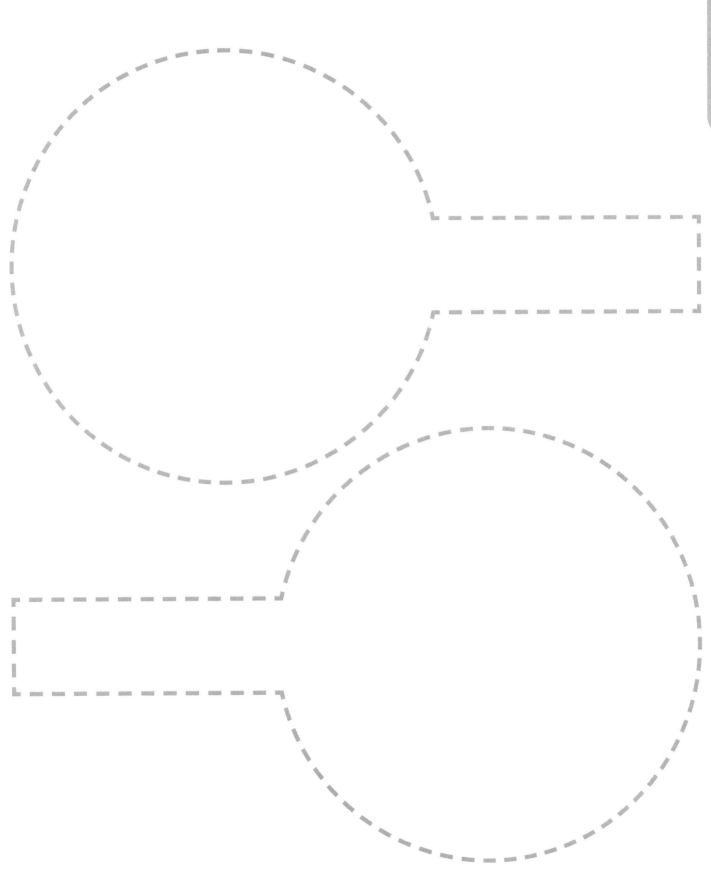

Two-box phoneme frame

Tog speaks in sound talk.

Break up words into sounds like Tog.

Three-box phoneme frame

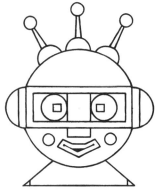

Tog speaks in sound talk.

Break up words into sounds like Tog.

Four-box phoneme frame

Say a word in sound talk.

Make the word on the **phoneme frame**.

Five-box phoneme frame

Say a word in sound talk.

Make the word on the **phoneme frame**.

Sort the words into two groups. Write or place the words on the correct post box.

From: **Sound Phonics: Teacher's Resource Book** by Carol Matchett (ISBN 978 07217 1224 6). Copyright © Schofield & Sims Ltd, 2014. Published by Schofield & Sims Ltd, Dogley Mill, Fenay Bridge, Huddersfield HD8 0NQ, UK (www.schofieldandsims.co.uk). This page may be photocopied after purchase for use within your school or institution only.

Sort the words into three groups. Write or place the words on the correct island.

From: **Sound Phonics: Teacher's Resource Book** by Carol Matchett (ISBN 978 07217 1224 6). Copyright © Schofield & Sims Ltd, 2014. Published by Schofield & Sims Ltd, Dogley Mill, Fenay Bridge, Huddersfield HD8 0NQ, UK (www.schofieldandsims.co.uk). This page may be photocopied after purchase for use within your school or institution only.

Sort the words into four groups. Write or place the words in the correct sack.

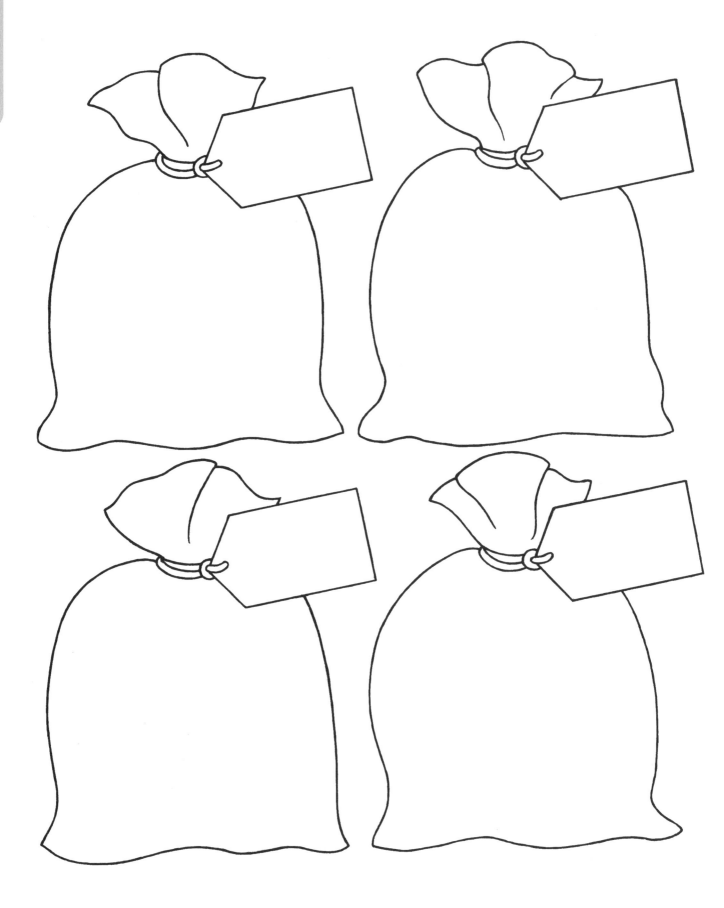

There is more than one spelling of the _____ sound.

Write a different spelling of this sound on each branch of this **phonic family tree**.

From: **Sound Phonics: Teacher's Resource Book** by Carol Matchett (ISBN 978 07217 1224 6). Copyright © Schofield & Sims Ltd, 2014. Published by Schofield & Sims Ltd, Dogley Mill,
Fenay Bridge, Huddersfield HD8 0NQ, UK (www.schofieldandsims.co.uk). This page may be photocopied after purchase for use within your school or institution only.

2

1

3

4

General resources

Phase Three
Book 2

my

you

was

they

all

her

are

Phase Four

said

so

no

do

like

have

some

come

Phase Four

were

there

little

one

what

when

out

Phase Five
Book 1

oh

people

Mr

Mrs

their

looked

called

asked

Phase Five
Book 2

would

could

should

where

who

many

any

water

work

Phase Five
Book 2

mouse

friend

thought

eyes

once

please

laughed

through

Activity book resources

All the resources in this section are intended for use with specific **Sound Phonics** activity books, and appropriate activity suggestions are provided in the **Teacher's Guide**. Page references relate to the corresponding activity book, rather than the **Teacher's Guide**.

Resources for Phase One

The resources for Phase One are sets of picture cards rather than words and sentences, and are designed for use mainly in adult-led activities. This reflects the oral nature of this Phase in *Letters and Sounds* and **Sound Phonics**. Most of the picture cards are organised by sound to reinforce rhyme, initial sounds and oral blending and segmenting. As the children will be quite young, you may wish to enlarge or laminate the cards to make them easier to handle.

Resources for Phases Two to Six

- *Sound mats* and *Tricky word mats* are a useful reference when recalling graphemes and tricky words. The children are encouraged to check the mats rather than choose an incorrect grapheme, and should gradually retain the correct spelling.

- *Games* provide pair or group activities to help the children practise their new phonic knowledge in an informal setting. The games are kept simple to avoid creating a distraction. The children should roll a dice, then say the sound of the graphemes they land on. If a child makes a mistake, he or she returns to the start.

- *Grapheme cards* can be used to introduce graphemes or practise recognition and recall. They show the grapheme, as well as a picture illustrating the sound it represents.

- *Word cards* and *Sound button words* contain the focus graphemes for each Phase, and can be used to practise blending and segmenting. In Phases Two to Four, some of the word cards have sound buttons. This allows you to adapt the resource to meet the needs of individual children. Confident blenders can use the word cards as they are, but it may be helpful to draw in the sound buttons for less confident children. In Phase Six the word cards are often base words to which suffixes or prefixes may be added.

- *Reading captions and sentences* contain words featuring known graphemes, and several sentences introduce new tricky words. Some are questions, clues, captions or speech, and may be used to introduce different sentence types. They can be read, cut up, illustrated or used as a model to build a new sentence. Many of the sentences have an accompanying set of *words to swap* that the children can use to create new sentences to read.

- *Phoneme frame letters* can be used with the phoneme frames to demonstrate or practise segmenting sounds to spell words. Lists of words that can be made with each set are included in the **Teacher's Guide**.

- *Reading and writing sentences*, *Phoneme spotting sentences* and *Sentence starters* allow the children to practise reading and spelling tricky words, eventually writing them in sentences of their own. Guidance on how to use these resources is provided in the **Teacher's Guide**.

Phase One

Phase One

Phase One

Phase One

From: **Sound Phonics: Teacher's Resource Book** by Carol Matchett (ISBN 978 07217 1224 6). Copyright © Schofield & Sims Ltd, 2014. Published by Schofield & Sims Ltd, Dogley Mill, Fenay Bridge, Huddersfield HD8 0NQ, UK (www.schofieldandsims.co.uk). This page may be photocopied after purchase for use within your school or institution only.

From: **Sound Phonics: Teacher's Resource Book** by Carol Matchett (ISBN 978 07217 1224 6). Copyright © Schofield & Sims Ltd, 2014. Published by Schofield & Sims Ltd, Dogley Mill, Fenay Bridge, Huddersfield HD8 0NQ, UK (www.schofieldandsims.co.uk). This page may be photocopied after purchase for use within your school or institution only.

Phase One

From: **Sound Phonics: Teacher's Resource Book** by Carol Matchett (ISBN 978 07217 1224 6). Copyright © Schofield & Sims Ltd, 2014. Published by Schofield & Sims Ltd, Dogley Mill, Fenay Bridge, Huddersfield HD8 0NQ, UK (www.schofieldandsims.co.uk). This page may be photocopied after purchase for use within your school or institution only.

From: **Sound Phonics: Teacher's Resource Book** by Carol Matchett (ISBN 978 07217 1224 6). Copyright © Schofield & Sims Ltd, 2014. Published by Schofield & Sims Ltd, Dogley Mill, Fenay Bridge, Huddersfield HD8 0NQ, UK (www.schofieldandsims.co.uk). *This page may be photocopied after purchase for use within your school or institution only.*

the to I go no

he she we me be

my you was they

all her are

Phases Two and Three

Cross the river on the stepping stones. Each time your counter lands on a letter, say the letter sound.

Start

Finish

From: **Sound Phonics: Teacher's Resource Book** by Carol Matchett (ISBN 978 07217 1224 6). Copyright © Schofield & Sims Ltd, 2014. Published by Schofield & Sims Ltd, Dogley Mill, Fenay Bridge, Huddersfield HD8 0NQ, UK (www.schofieldandsims.co.uk). This page may be photocopied after purchase for use within your school or institution only.

 Ss

 a

 t

 p

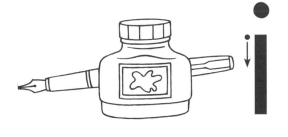 i

 n

 m

 d

Phase Two

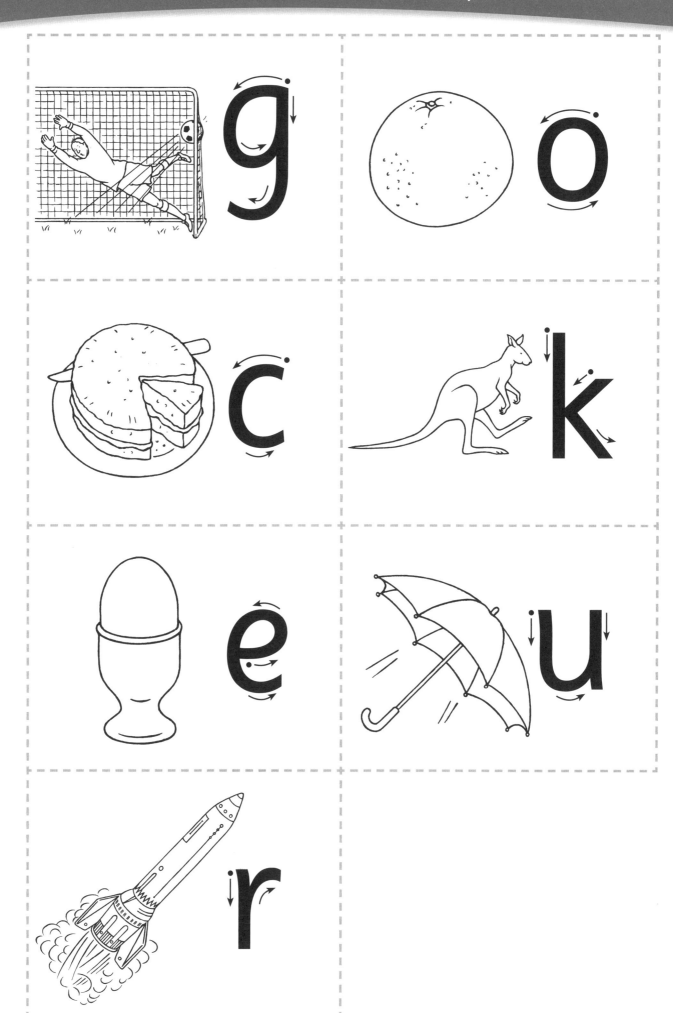

From: **Sound Phonics: Teacher's Resource Book** by Carol Matchett (ISBN 978 07217 1224 6). Copyright © Schofield & Sims Ltd, 2014. Published by Schofield & Sims Ltd, Dogley Mill, Fenay Bridge, Huddersfield HD8 0NQ, UK (www.schofieldandsims.co.uk). This page may be photocopied after purchase for use within your school or institution only.

From: *Sound Phonics: Teacher's Resource Book* by Carol Matchett (ISBN 978 07217 1224 6). Copyright © Schofield & Sims Ltd, 2014. Published by Schofield & Sims Ltd, Dogley Mill,
Fenay Bridge, Huddersfield HD8 0NQ, UK (www.schofieldandsims.co.uk). This page may be photocopied after purchase for use within your school or institution only.

Phase Two

Sets 1–3 (pages 18, 24)

d	g	t	p
s	a	i	o

Sets 1–4 (page 30)

d	g	t	u
r	e	n	m

Sets 1–5 (page 40)

b	g	t	u
r	e	n	l

blending: Set 1, i, n page 10	blending: Sets 1 and 2 page 14	blending: g, o page 17	blending: c, k page 22
it	am	pot	cot
tin	map	dog	cop
sat	sad	pop	kid
pan	dip	tag	Kim
tap	did	nag	cod
pat	din	dig	cog
sip	mad	pig	kit

Phase Two

blending: e page 26	blending: Sets 1 to 4 page 29	blending: h, b page 35	blending: l, f page 39
get ●●●	run ●●●	hut ●●●	fit ●●●
ten ●●●	cup ●●●	hop ●●●	fan ●●●
met ●●●	sun ●●●	hum ●●●	fat ●●●
men ●●●	set ●●●	hug ●●●	fig ●●●
set ●●●	rim ●●●	bit ●●●	leg ●●●
den ●●●	rip ●●●	bad ●●●	lit ●●●
ted ●●●	red ●●●	bed ●●●	lad ●●●

Phase Two

Reading caption with words to swap: **and** (page 23)

Dad	and	Kim

Nan	Tom	Sam	a dog
a cat	Pam	Ken	a man

Reading caption with words to swap: **the** (page 32)

Sid	in	the	mud

Sam	Sit	Mog	sun
on	rug	mat	den

From: **Sound Phonics: Teacher's Resource Book** *by Carol Matchett (ISBN 978 07217 1224 6). Copyright © Schofield & Sims Ltd, 2014. Published by Schofield & Sims Ltd, Dogley Mill, Fenay Bridge, Huddersfield HD8 0NQ, UK (www.schofieldandsims.co.uk). This page may be photocopied after purchase for use within your school or institution only.*

Phase Two

Reading sign with words to swap: **to** (page 36)

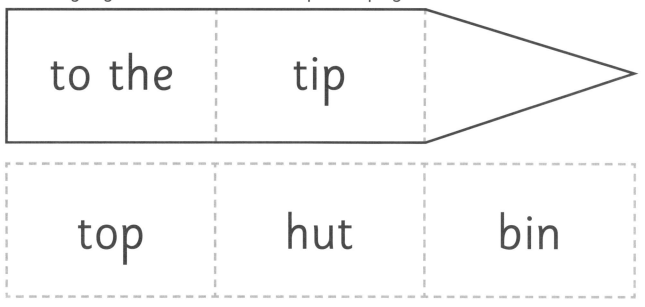

to the	tip

top	hut	bin

Reading sentence with words to swap: **I** (page 41)

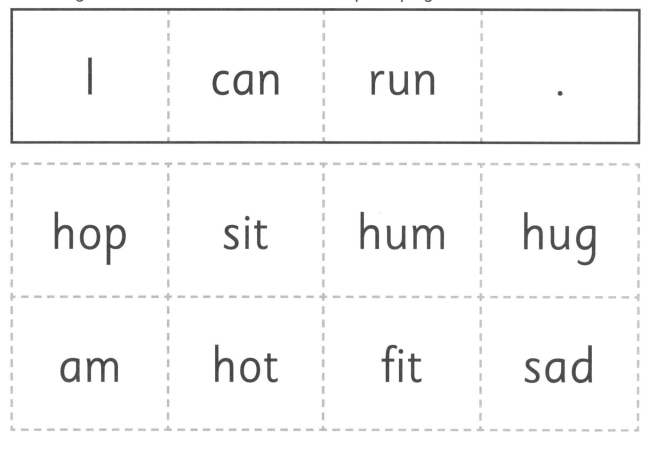

I	can	run	.

hop	sit	hum	hug
am	hot	fit	sad

From: **Sound Phonics: Teacher's Resource Book** by Carol Matchett (ISBN 978 07217 1224 6). Copyright © Schofield & Sims Ltd, 2014. Published by Schofield & Sims Ltd, Dogley Mill, Fenay Bridge, Huddersfield HD8 0NQ, UK (www.schofieldandsims.co.uk). This page may be photocopied after purchase for use within your school or institution only.

Phase Two

Reading caption with words to swap: **no** (page 42)

no	hat	on the	peg

cap	bag	man	bus
cat	mat	lid	pan

Reading note with words to swap: **go** (page 43)

go and get the	map

bag	bus	cup
bin	top	bit

Phase Two

Phase Three

Race to the stars! When your counter lands on a star, read and say the sound.

Blast off!

Finish

Phase Three

Use counters to race your partner up the beanstalk. When you land on a leaf, read and say the word.

Phase Three

Cut out the cards. See how many words you can read before the timer runs out.

on	them	can	now
Dad	with	had	see
off	Mum	back	for
then	of	and	down
get	this	him	look
not	that	his	too
but	up	big	will
got	is	if	put

Phase Three

Note: further **Against the clock** words can be found at the end of the *Phase Four* resources. These should be added for practice in *Phase Four* and beyond.

j

v

w

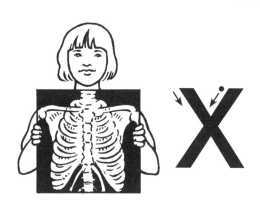
x

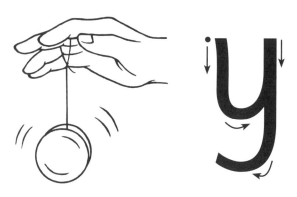
y

z

qu

zz

sh

ng

th

ch

ff

ll

ss

ck

From: *Sound Phonics: Teacher's Resource Book* by Carol Matchett (ISBN 978 07217 1224 6). Copyright © Schofield & Sims Ltd, 2014. Published by Schofield & Sims Ltd, Dogley Mill, Fenay Bridge, Huddersfield HD8 0NQ, UK (www.schofieldandsims.co.uk). This page may be photocopied after purchase for use within your school or institution only.

Sets 1–6 (page 16)

b	o	e	t
j	v	w	i

sh and ch (page 29)

d	n	ll	p
sh	ch	i	e

th and ng (page 34)

p	w	t	s
th	ng	i	a

blending: Sets 1 to 5 page 5	endings: ss, ll, ff page 7	ending: ck page 8	blending: Set 6 page 15
pit	hiss	kick	jam
tan	fuss	pick	jog
gas	mess	pack	van
bud	tell	sick	wag
pop	fill	rock	web
rib	huff	back	wax
had	cuff	dock	six

From: **Sound Phonics: Teacher's Resource Book** by Carol Matchett (ISBN 978 07217 1224 6). Copyright © Schofield & Sims Ltd, 2014. Published by Schofield & Sims Ltd, Dogley Mill, Fenay Bridge, Huddersfield HD8 0NQ, UK (www.schofieldandsims.co.uk). This page may be photocopied after purchase for use within your school or institution only.

Phase Three Book 1

blending: Set 7 page 21	blending: sh page 27	blending: ch page 28	blending: th, ng page 33
yes	fish	chin	moth
yet	cash	chug	thud
yum	hush	rich	path
zip	bash	chat	ring
quiz	shed	chill	rang
quit	shot	check	wing
yell	shell	chick	sing

Phase Three Book 1

Reading sentence with words to swap: **no** (page 9)

| No | duck | can | kick | . |

| hiss | peck | tell | hum |

| pig | rat | sock | bell |

Reading sentence with words to swap: **go**, **to**, **the** (page 17)

| I can | go | to get the | jam | . |

| box | bus | bell | jet |

| run | jog | boss | doll |

Phase Three Book 1

Reading sentence with words to swap: **he**, **she** (page 30)

He	can fix the	van	.

Tess	Jack	Jill	shed
Mick	She	zip	ship

Reading caption with words to swap: **my** (page 40)

This	is	my	fish	.

Mum	Dad	dog	rabbit
bed	den	ring	laptop

From: **Sound Phonics: Teacher's Resource Book** by Carol Matchett (ISBN 978 07217 1224 6). Copyright © Schofield & Sims Ltd, 2014. Published by Schofield & Sims Ltd, Dogley Mill, Fenay Bridge, Huddersfield HD8 0NQ, UK (www.schofieldandsims.co.uk). This page may be photocopied after purchase for use within your school or institution only.

Reading question: **will** (page 23)

Will the sun fit in a box?

Reading clue: **this, with, them** (page 36)

This dog digs with them.

Reading questions: **we, be, me** (page 38)

Can we be quick?

Is a jet as quick as me?

Phase Three Book 2

 ai

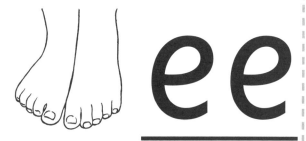 ee

 igh

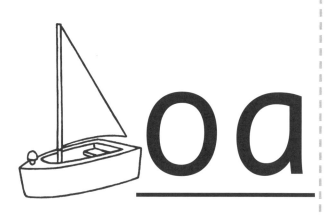 oa

 oo

oo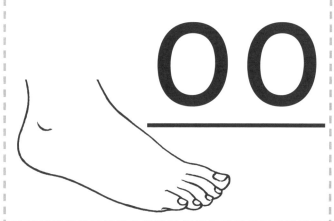

 ar

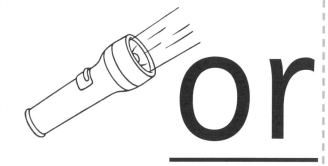 or

ur

ow

oi

ear

air

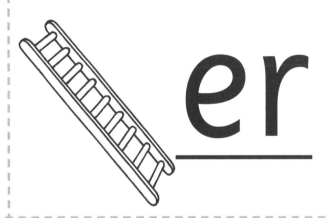
er

ure

Note: *the grapheme* **ure** *is not specifically practised in* **Sound Phonics** *because the children are unlikely to encounter many words with this sound. However, a grapheme card is included so teachers can introduce it if they wish, using words such as p***ure***, c***ure*** *and s***ure***.*

Phase Three Book 2

ai and ee (page 9)

l	r	k	p
s	d	ai	ee

oa and oo (page 18)

b	f	r	d
t	l	oa	oo

ar, or and ur (page 27)

f	k	c	p
t	ar	or	ur

blending: ai page 6	blending: ee page 8	blending: igh page 11	blending: oa page 13
nail	feed	high	coat
gain	see	light	road
hail	need	night	soap
aim	deep	fight	goat
main	feet	thigh	soak
paid	keep	tights	foal
tail	seen	right	boat

Phase Three Book 2

blending: oo page 17	blending: oo page 17	blending: ar page 21	blending: or page 23
boot	look	bark	cord
hoof	foot	card	fork
zoom	good	cart	cork
cool	book	car	sort
food	wood	jar	worn
moon	hook	hard	short
roof	wool	park	for

blending: ur page 26	blending: ow page 29	blending: oi page 31	blending: ear page 35
fur	owl	join	fear
curl	gown	coin	gear
burn	town	foil	tear
church	pow	oil	beard
churn	cow	toil	shear

blending: air page 37	blending: er page 40	blending: er page 40	ure
fair	singer	rocker	pure
hair	power	farmer	cure
lair	boxer	letter	sure

Note: *the grapheme* **ure** *is not specifically practised in* **Sound Phonics** *because the children are unlikely to encounter many words with this sound. However, a grapheme card is included so teachers can introduce it if they wish, using words such as* p**ure***,* c**ure** *and* s**ure***.*

Reading question with words to swap: **you** (page 14)

Can you see	hail	?

rain	pain	light

Reading sentence with words to swap: **was** (page 24)

The	boat	was in the	port.

car	goat	cart	jeep
yard	wood	barn	road

From: **Sound Phonics: Teacher's Resource Book** by Carol Matchett (ISBN 978 07217 1224 6). Copyright © Schofield & Sims Ltd, 2014. Published by Schofield & Sims Ltd, Dogley Mill, Fenay Bridge, Huddersfield HD8 0NQ, UK (www.schofieldandsims.co.uk). This page may be photocopied after purchase for use within your school or institution only.

Reading clues: **they** (page 32)

they can howl

they can woof

they can bark

Reading question with words to swap: **all** (page 38)

| Can you all | sigh | ? |

| howl | hoot | sing | march |

| sail | fish | cook | surf |

*From: **Sound Phonics: Teacher's Resource Book** by Carol Matchett (ISBN 978 07217 1224 6). Copyright © Schofield & Sims Ltd, 2014. Published by Schofield & Sims Ltd, Dogley Mill, Fenay Bridge, Huddersfield HD8 0NQ, UK (www.schofieldandsims.co.uk). This page may be photocopied after purchase for use within your school or institution only.*

Phase Three Book 2

Reading sentence with words to swap: **his**, **her** (page 41)

Liz	lost	her	socks	.

Josh	Jill	Mark	his
book	torch	jacket	hood

Reading sentence with words to swap: **are** (page 42)

Thorns	are	sharp	.

food	quick	hard	rich
Teeth	Kings	Cars	Chips

From: **Sound Phonics: Teacher's Resource Book** by Carol Matchett (ISBN 978 07217 1224 6). Copyright © Schofield & Sims Ltd, 2014. Published by Schofield & Sims Ltd, Dogley Mill, Fenay Bridge, Huddersfield HD8 0NQ, UK (www.schofieldandsims.co.uk). This page may be photocopied after purchase for use within your school or institution only.

two-part words Phase Three Book 2 page 19	two-part words Phase Three Book 2 page 33	two-part words Phase Four page 26	two-part words Phase Four page 38
moonlight	tinfoil	postman	handstand
bedroom	carpet	milkman	weekend
tonight	farmyard	dustbin	waistband
cookbook	churchyard	hairbrush	upstairs
footpath	popcorn	handbag	driftwood
mailbox	morning	earring	waistcoat
sixteen	market	grasshopper	thunderstorm

From: **Sound Phonics: Teacher's Resource Book** by Carol Matchett (ISBN 978 07217 1224 6). Copyright © Schofield & Sims Ltd, 2014. Published by Schofield & Sims Ltd, Dogley Mill, Fenay Bridge, Huddersfield HD8 0NQ, UK (www.schofieldandsims.co.uk). This page may be photocopied after purchase for use within your school or institution only.

Phase Four

said have like

so come one

some

were there little

do when out what

Race your partner to the top of the chimney. When your counter lands on a brick, read and say the word.

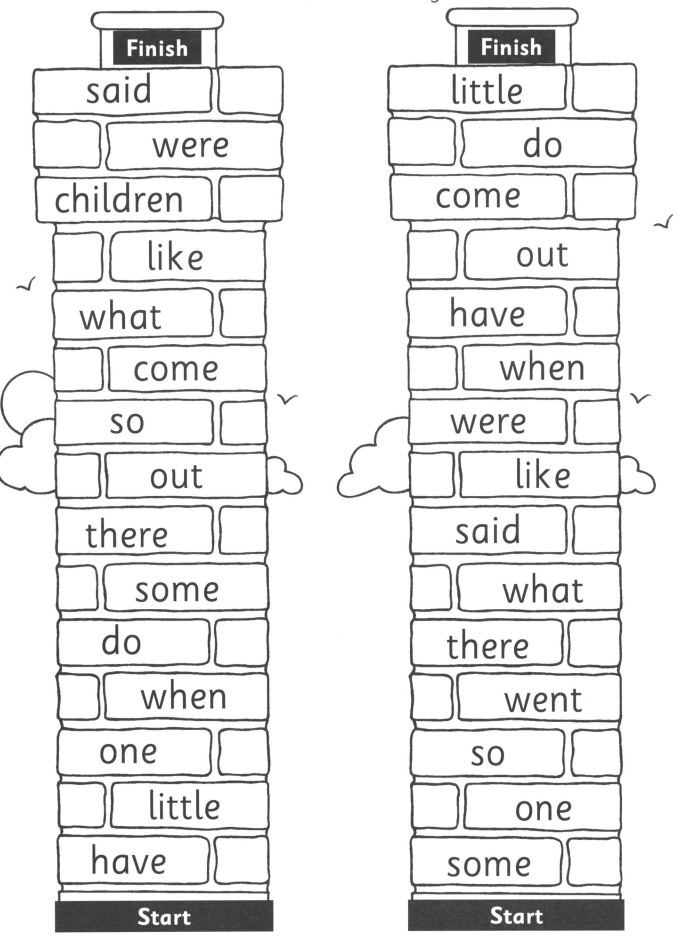

Finish

said

were

children

like

what

come

so

out

there

some

do

when

one

little

have

Start

Finish

little

do

come

out

have

when

were

like

said

what

there

went

so

one

some

Start

Phase Four

From: **Sound Phonics: Teacher's Resource Book** by Carol Matchett (ISBN 978 07217 1224 6). Copyright © Schofield & Sims Ltd, 2014. Published by Schofield & Sims Ltd, Dogley Mill, Fenay Bridge, Huddersfield HD8 0NQ, UK (www.schofieldandsims.co.uk).

CVCC (page 12)

d	n	s	b	h
t	l	a	e	k

CCVC (page 19)

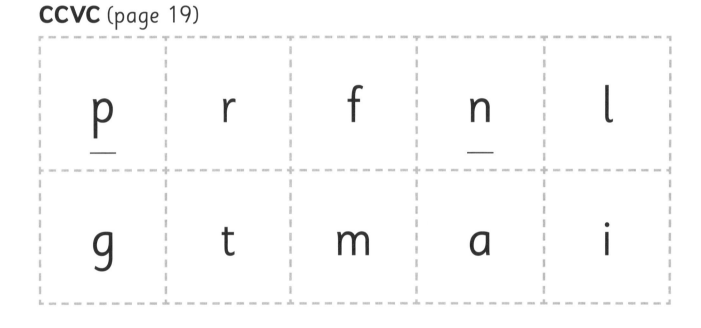

p	r	f	n	l
g	t	m	a	i

CVCC and **CCVC** (page 31)

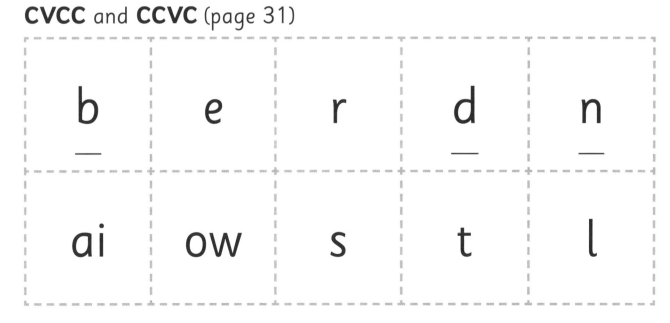

b	e	r	d	n
ai	ow	s	t	l

Phase Four

blending: CVCC page 10	blending: CVCC page 11	blending: CCVC page 17	blending: CCVC page 18
dent	help	snap	pram
went	jump	flag	plot
land	gift	club	grin
pond	next	flat	drop
cost	damp	trap	trick
best	soft	crack	swim
hand	tuft	click	blob

Phase Four

Phase Four

blending: CVCC, CCVC page 22	blending: CCVC page 29	blending: CVCC, CCVC page 30	blending: CCVCC page 35
chomp	steep	groan	print
punch	sweep	bleed	stand
chimp	spear	clown	twist
sting	spoon	creep	frost
thrush	smart	boost	grunt
thank	spoil	toast	slept
chest	sleek	float	plump

Reading speech: **said** (page 13)

"I lost my sheep," she said.

"Is this my tent?" he said.

Reading sentence with words to swap: **so** (page 15)

Mark is	fast	and so am I.

rich	good	lost
short	keen	fair

Reading question with words to swap: **do** (page 20)

Do	taps	drip	?

ducks	frogs	fish	flags
jump	swim	flap	croak

Reading sentence with words to swap: **like** (page 21)

I	like	to	swim	.

cook	help	jump	clap
chat	sing	fish	camp

Phase Four

Reading sentence with words to swap: **have** (page 23)

Frogs	have	legs	.

Sharks	Owls	Chimps	Cows
teeth	tails	wings	Moths

Reading caption with words to swap: **little** (page 33)

the	little	red	hen

green	brown	frog	train
boat	truck	drum	owl

Phase Four

Reading sentence with words to swap: **some**, **come** (page 24)

| Some | plums | come in packs of six. |
| eggs | flags | cards | forks |

Reading sentence with words to swap: **there**, **were** (page 32)

| There were three | trees | on the hill |
| tents | tracks | flags | goats |

Reading question: **what** (page 37)

What can we see on a clear night?

Reading question with words to swap: **when** (page 40)

When do you | see | the | sun?

stars	wind
fog	feel
moon	
rain	

From: **Sound Phonics: Teacher's Resource Book** by Carol Matchett (ISBN 978 07217 1224 6). Copyright © Schofield & Sims Ltd, 2014. Published by Schofield & Sims Ltd, Dogley Mill, Fenay Bridge, Huddersfield HD8 0NQ, UK (www.schofieldandsims.co.uk). This page may be photocopied after purchase for use within your school or institution only.

Reading caption with words to swap: **one** (page 36)

one	spoon	in the	dish

plum	tree	pond	rock
chimp	thrush	owl	sink

Reading sentence with words to swap: **out** (page 42)

He	fell	out	of the	tree	.

She	We	jumps	bunk
pram	cart	boat	train

Against the clock cards (see Phase Three resources)

went	from	just	help

*From: **Sound Phonics: Teacher's Resource Book** by Carol Matchett (ISBN 978 07217 1224 6). Copyright © Schofield & Sims Ltd, 2014. Published by Schofield & Sims Ltd, Dogley Mill, Fenay Bridge, Huddersfield HD8 0NQ, UK (www.schofieldandsims.co.uk). This page may be photocopied after purchase for use within your school or institution only.*

oy

oe

ph

a-e / u-e

ea

ew

e-i / i-e

ie

ue

wh

o-e / a-o

ou

ir / aw

ey

a-e / e-e

ay

au

From: *Sound Phonics: Teacher's Resource Book* by Carol Matchett (ISBN 978 07217 1224 6). Copyright © Schofield & Sims Ltd, 2014. Published by Schofield & Sims Ltd, Dogley Mill, Fenay Bridge, Huddersfield HD8 0NQ, UK (www.schofieldandsims.co.uk). This page may be photocopied after purchase for use within your school or institution only.

Phase Five

oh people Mr Mrs their

looked called asked

would could should what

where who many any

water work mouse friend

thought eyes once please

laughed through

How much gold can you win? When your counter lands on a coin, read and say the sound.

Start

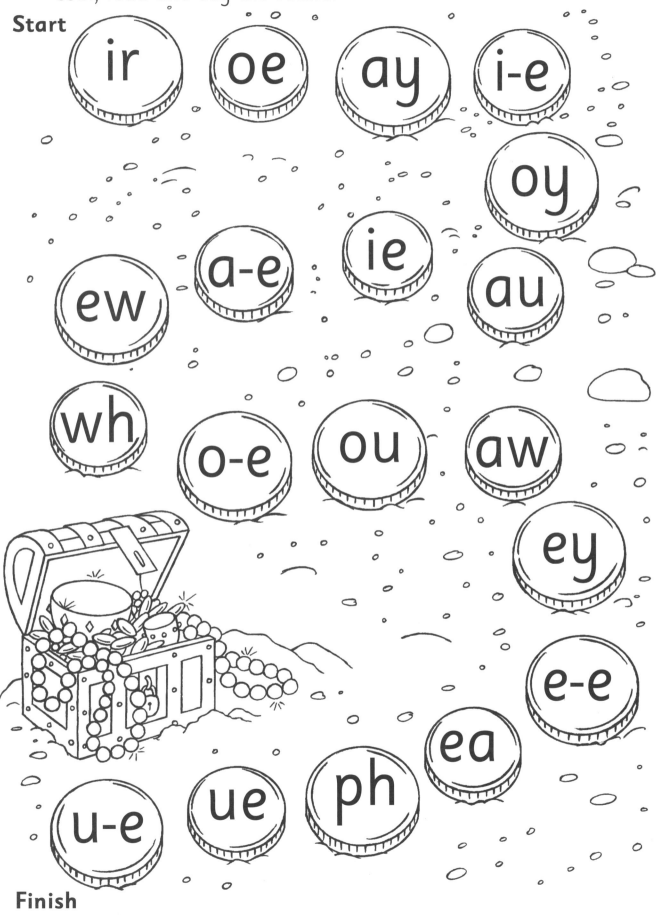

Finish

Find your way out of the maze. When you pass a word you must read it or go back to the start.

Start

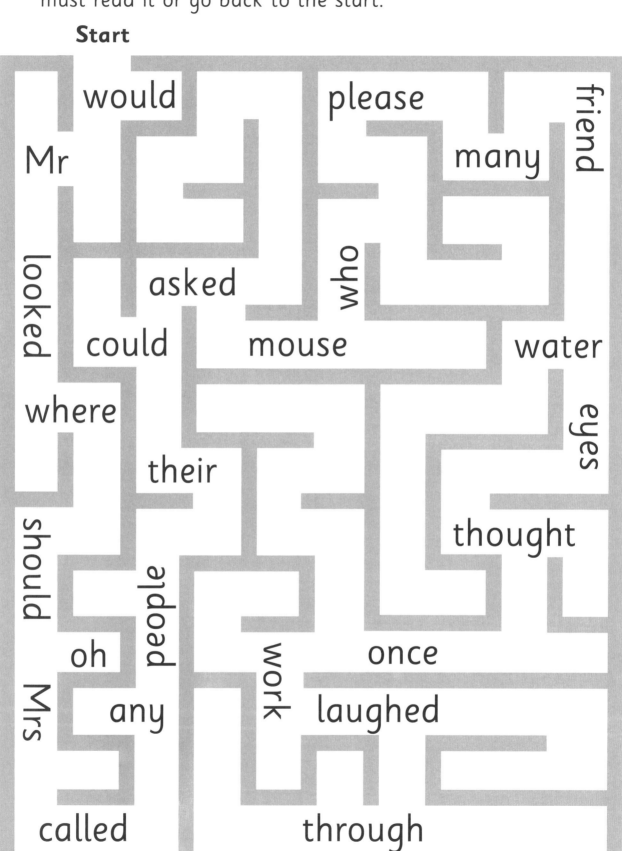

would — please — friend
Mr — many
looked — asked — who
could — mouse — water
where — eyes
their — thought
should — people
oh — work — once
Mrs — any — laughed
called — through

Finish

From: **Sound Phonics: Teacher's Resource Book** by Carol Matchett (ISBN 978 07217 1224 6). Copyright © Schofield & Sims Ltd, 2014. Published by Schofield & Sims Ltd, Dogley Mill, Fenay Bridge, Huddersfield HD8 0NQ, UK (www.schofieldandsims.co.uk). This page may be photocopied after purchase for use within your school or institution only.

Phase Five

 ay

 ou

 ie

 ea

 oy

 ir

 aw

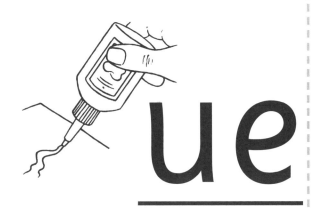 ue

Phase Five Book 1

 ew

 oe

 au

 ey

 a-e

 e-e

 i-e

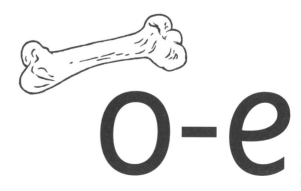 o-e

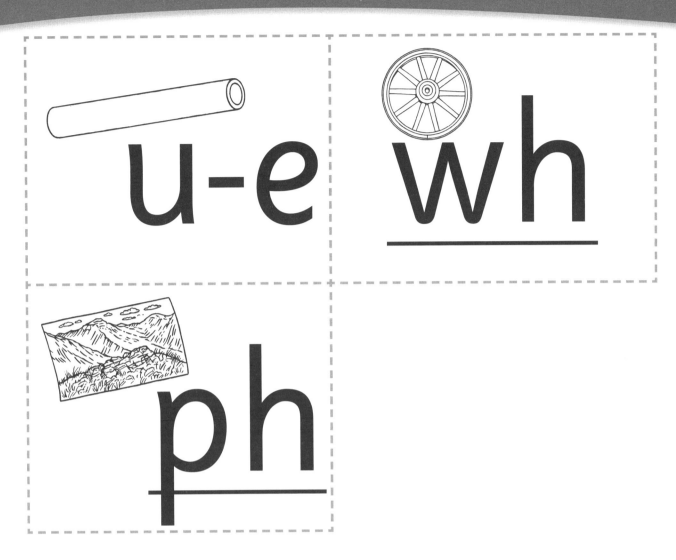

u-e   wh

ph

Phoneme frame letters (page 13)

b	s	m	ch
ea	t	n	l

*From: **Sound Phonics: Teacher's Resource Book** by Carol Matchett (ISBN 978 07217 1224 6). Copyright © Schofield & Sims Ltd, 2014. Published by Schofield & Sims Ltd, Dogley Mill, Fenay Bridge, Huddersfield HD8 0NQ, UK (www.schofieldandsims.co.uk). This page may be photocopied after purchase for use within your school or institution only.*

grapheme: ay page 9	grapheme: ou page 10	grapheme: ie page 11	grapheme: ea page 12
say	out	die	eat
day	about	lies	read
pay	found	tried	heap
play	loud	spied	least
stray	sound	toy	steam
pray	round	Roy	beach
sway	proud	annoy	speak
away	mount	cowboy	real

grapheme: oy
page 17

grapheme: ir page 18	grapheme: aw page 19	grapheme: ue page 20	grapheme: ew page 24
sir	paw	clue	chew
skirt	raw	blue	blew
third	claw	Sue	grew
stir	jaw	glue	flew
swirl	lawn		threw
firm	yawn	toes	drew
dirt	draw	Joe	crew
twirl	law	woe	new

grapheme: oe page 25

Phase Five Book 1

grapheme: a-e page 30	grapheme: i-e page 32	grapheme: o-e page 33	grapheme: u-e page 34
came	like	home	June
made	time	pole	rule
same	nice	hope	cube
make	ripe	froze	huge
game	shine	those	tune
race	prize	woke	duke
snake	wide	vote	cute
date	smile	throne	tube

Phase Five Book 1

Reading speech with words to swap: **oh** (page 8)

"Oh dear, I have lost my scarf ."

crown	slipper	growl	lamp
tooth	hood	cloak	trunk

Reading sentence with words to swap: **Mr**, **Mrs** (page 21)

Mr Smith has a blue shirt .

Mrs	Parks	green	scarf
skirt	shawl	dress	jumper

Phase Five Book 1

Phase Five Book 1

Reading question: **people** (page 14)

Can people land on the moon?

Reading sentence: **their** (page 28)

The twins keep their toys in the chest.

Reading sentence with words to swap: **ed** words (page 36)

I	looked	for	help	.

called	asked	Mum
Eve	June	Pete

Reading questions: **wh** words (page 41)

What is blue?

Where can you keep fish?

When do you sleep?

From: **Sound Phonics: Teacher's Resource Book** by Carol Matchett (ISBN 978 07217 1224 6). Copyright © Schofield & Sims Ltd, 2014. Published by Schofield & Sims Ltd, Dogley Mill, Fenay Bridge, Huddersfield HD8 0NQ, UK (www.schofieldandsims.co.uk). This page may be photocopied after purchase for use within your school or institution only.

Writing caption: **some** (page 16)

some beads on a string

Writing speech: **come**, **said** (page 22)

"Come with me," said Roy.

Writing sentence: **have** (page 29)

Some grapes have pips.

Writing sentence: **were**, **there** (page 38)

There were five names on the list.

Writing sentence: **go**, **do**, **like** (page 42)

I do like to go to the park.

From: **Sound Phonics: Teacher's Resource Book** by Carol Matchett (ISBN 978 07217 1224 6). Copyright © Schofield & Sims Ltd, 2014. Published by Schofield & Sims Ltd, Dogley Mill, Fenay Bridge, Huddersfield HD8 0NQ, UK (www.schofieldandsims.co.uk). This page may be photocopied after purchase for use within your school or institution only.

two-part words Phase Five Book 1 page 15	two-part words Phase Five Book 1 page 37	two-part words Phase Five Book 2 pages 9, 10
tearoom	seaside	thirteen
daylight	sunshine	whisper
magpie	bookcase	clockwise
seaweed	outside	toothpaste
peanut	rescue	somewhere
Sunday	statue	bagpipes
playground	escape	basement
crayon	bonfire	scrapbook

Phase Five Books 1 and 2

pronunciations: i page 12	pronunciations: o page 13	pronunciations: e page 14	pronunciations: u page 15
find	gold	he	unit
blink	cloth	west	crunch
blind	hold	we	music
shrink	soft	swept	plump
mild	most	smelt	truth
thrill	lost	began	crush
grind	sold	become	stupid
children	shock	invent	punish
slim	post		
behind	across		

pronunciations: c page 18	pronunciations: g page 19	pronunciations: ow page 24	pronunciations: ow page 24
ice	magic	brown	slow
coast	gloat	brow	show
dance	gent	allow	below
picnic	grave	drown	glow
pencil	age	crowd	crow
cope	groan	towel	blow
circus	strange	flower	follow
cactus	target	shower	own
princess	large	tower	throw
crime	dagger	growl	yellow

Phase Five Book 2

pronunciations: ie page 25	pronunciations: ea page 26	pronunciations: er page 27	homographs page 32
tie	head	never	bow
field	dread	silver	row
pie	feather	river	read
chief	instead	sister	wind
magpie	health	over	tear
shield	wealth	term	lead
died	weather	herbs	live
belief	beast	jerk	close
lies	treat	perch	wound
	please	herself	polish

Phase Five Book 2

pronunciations: y page 33	pronunciations: a page 34	pronunciations: ch page 36	pronunciations: ou page 37
cry	after	choke	shout
dry	grand	drench	mouth
fry	traffic	cheese	ground
sly	grasp	richer	south
sky	danger	chef	ouch
story	bacon	Michelle	mould
body	wash	Chris	soup
penny	wasp	school	youth
thirty	wand	aches	could
year	wallet	chemist	

Phase Five Book 2

Reading question with words to swap: **would**, **could**, **should** (page 11)

Would	you	eat	sprouts	?

Could	Should	peas	meat
crusts	fish	straw	grass

Reading question with words to swap: **who**, **what** (page 21)

Who	might you see at a	circus	?

What	market	zoo	farm
fair	wedding	port	track

From: **Sound Phonics: Teacher's Resource Book** by Carol Matchett (ISBN 978 07217 1224 6). Copyright © Schofield & Sims Ltd, 2014. Published by Schofield & Sims Ltd, Dogley Mill, Fenay Bridge, Huddersfield HD8 0NQ, UK (www.schofieldandsims.co.uk). This page may be photocopied after purchase for use within your school or institution only.

Reading sentence: **i**, **o**, **e**, **u** (page 16)

> # Tog is a robot not a human being.

Reading sentence: **ow**, **ea** (page 29)

> # The clown was ready to put on a show.

Reading sentence: homographs (page 32)

> # The wind blew.
>
> # Wind up the yoyo.

Reading sentence: **ch**, **a**, **y** (page 39)

> # What might the chef fry the lady for her lunch?

From: **Sound Phonics: Teacher's Resource Book** by Carol Matchett (ISBN 978 07217 1224 6). Copyright © Schofield & Sims Ltd, 2014. Published by Schofield & Sims Ltd, Dogley Mill, Fenay Bridge, Huddersfield HD8 0NQ, UK (www.schofieldandsims.co.uk). This page may be photocopied after purchase for use within your school or institution only.

Reading question with words to swap: **any**, **many** (page 30)

| Do you have | any | pets | ? |

| many | win | books | toys |
| cows | sisters | prizes | races |

Reading question with words to swap: **water**, **work** (page 40)

| Do | boats | work in | water | ? |

| crayons | clocks | sand |

Story sentence: **mouse**, **friend**, **thought** (page 41)

| Town Mouse thought he would visit his friend Field Mouse. |

Story sentence: **eyes**, **once** (page 42)

> # There was once a monster with big round eyes.

Story sentence: **laughed**, **through** (page 43)

> # A grasshopper laughed her way through summer.

Writing sentences: **so** (page 17)

> # The turnip was so big.

Writing captions: **little** (page 22)

> # the little blue digger

Writing questions: **what** (page 35)

> # What time is it?

From: **Sound Phonics: Teacher's Resource Book** by Carol Matchett (ISBN 978 07217 1224 6). Copyright © Schofield & Sims Ltd, 2014. Published by Schofield & Sims Ltd, Dogley Mill, Fenay Bridge, Huddersfield HD8 0NQ, UK (www.schofieldandsims.co.uk). This page may be photocopied after purchase for use within your school or institution only.

Phase Five Book 3

spellings: w sound page 5	spellings: ch sound page 8	spellings: m sound page 9	spellings: n sound page 10
whale	pitch	dumb	knee
whisper	switch	bomb	knew
whisker	snatch	numb	knob
which	hatch	thumb	knot
while	sketch	limb	kneel
why	clutch	storm	sign
where	punch	harm	note
whack	lunch	broom	new
witch	bunch	cream	need
wipe	rich	zoom	none

Phase Five Book 3

spellings: v sound page 14	spellings: j sound page 15	spellings: s sound page 16	spellings: o sound page 19
give	wedge	mouse	want
nerve	sledge	horse	watch
serve	hedge	grease	wand
swerve	edge	purse	what
starve	badge	loose	wasp
carve	nudge	bristle	swan
drive	lodge	glisten	swap
glove	dodge	rustle	swat
weave	barge	bustle	
sleeve	urge	least	

Phase Five Book 3

two-part words page 34	spellings: or sound page 36	spellings: ear sound page 40	spellings: air sound page 41
lolly	scorn	dear	airport
puppy	snort	year	hairs
fifty	cornet	rear	upstairs
jelly	lord	spear	swear
story	fourteen	fears	tear
baby	yours	beer	scare
monkey	chalk	steer	glare
honey	tall	deer	spare
jockey	fall	queer	stare
valley	wall	cheer	bare

Phoneme spotting: **f** sound (page 6)

I took a fine photo of the flag flying off the pole.

Phoneme spotting: **c** sound (page 7)

A cat and a kangaroo came to school in a sack.

Phoneme spotting: **r** sound (page 11)

Rob wrote a story about a ruby ring lost under a rock.

Phoneme spotting: **e** sound (page 18)

Ben is ready to help steady the red tent.

From: Sound Phonics: Teacher's Resource Book by Carol Matchett (ISBN 978 07217 1224 6). Copyright © Schofield & Sims Ltd, 2014. Published by Schofield & Sims Ltd, Dogley Mill, Fenay Bridge, Huddersfield HD8 0NQ, UK (www.schofieldandsims.co.uk). This page may be photocopied after purchase for use within your school or institution only.

Phoneme spotting: **long a** sound (page 21)

Jake paid for the grapes but left the tray in the rain all day.

Phoneme spotting: **long ee** sound (page 23)

I need beans and a swede from the heap in the field.

Phoneme spotting: **long i** sound (page 25)

I will tie a string to the kite and try to fly it up high.

Phoneme spotting: **long o** sound (page 28)

My toes froze as I dug a hole in the load of snow.

Phoneme spotting: **long oo** sound (page 31)

Is it true there is a new moon in June?

Phoneme spotting: **ur** sound (page 37)

The girl on the kerb turned round when she heard the leaves whirl in the wind.

Phoneme spotting: **ow** sound (page 38)

I found the brown cow about to jump over the cloud.

Phoneme spotting: **oi** sound (page 39)

The boy enjoys peeling the foil off the coin.

Sentence starter with words to swap: **looked**, **called**, **asked** (page 13)

The	teacher	looked	for ...

thief	prince	giant
called	asked	children

Sentence starter with words to swap: **Mr**, **Mrs** (page 27)

Mr	Blake	is ...

Mrs	Jones	Carter	Brown
has	will	can	was

Sentence starter: **their**, **people** (page 35)

Some people like their ...

boiled	fresh	eggs	fried
tea	strong	weak	on toast

spellings: wor page 11	counting syllables page 19	shortened words pages 22–23	adding es page 25
words	alphabet	let's	pie
worm	October	he's	card
worker	Thursday	hasn't	toy
worse	elbow	didn't	screw
worthy	yesterday	isn't	spark
world	afternoon	I'd	fish
worry	envelope	she's	lash
were	explode	we've	watch
wolf	urgent	we'll	match
	rescue		cross
	misbehave		dress
	altogether		kiss

Phase Six Book 1

Phase Six Book 1

adding s or es page 27	adding ed page 29	adding ed page 30	adding ed page 31
chatter	yawn	shock	point
moan	sail	reach	boast
creep	moan	hiss	lift
spring	dream	peep	need
growl	sigh	blink	melt
doze	snow	brush	blast
race	clean	stamp	dust
march	train	cook	plant
fuss	drown	wash	act
crash	pull	stoop	dent
stretch			
rush			

Phase Six Book 1

adding ed page 35	adding ed page 36	adding ing page 40	adding ing page 41
boil	peel	fight	wait
serve	flap	slide	trot
soak	dart	paint	join
rule	plan	shine	win
reach	treat	count	keep
blame	drop	use	slip
open	load	howl	steam
hate	tug	close	swim
hunt	moan	burst	weep
choke	prod	skate	sob
talk	float	wink	boil
skate	stun	shave	tug

Introducing '**w special**' words (pages 10–11)

Did the wasp want a wash?

Did the worm give his word?

Introducing shortened words (page 22)

I don't go fast.
In fact, I'm very slow.

I've got a shell. It's on my back.

Introducing **ing** endings: The ing rhyme (page 39)

Polly is playing
Dan is dreaming
Rob is reading
Sam is screaming.

Introducing **ed** endings (page 28)

The red balloon

Yesterday, a red balloon floated up, up and away.

A lady pointed at it. A dog barked at it. Ducks quacked at it. The farmer shouted at it.

As it drifted on and on, lots of people peered at it.

Then the balloon landed in a park. All the children played with it and the balloon was very happy.

From: **Sound Phonics: Teacher's Resource Book** by Carol Matchett (ISBN 978 07217 1224 6). Copyright © Schofield & Sims Ltd, 2014. Published by Schofield & Sims Ltd, Dogley Mill, Fenay Bridge, Huddersfield HD8 0NQ, UK (www.schofieldandsims.co.uk). This page may be photocopied after purchase for use within your school or institution only.

Phase Six Book 1

Writing sentence: **please**, **water** (page 12)

Please fetch me a cup of water.

Writing sentence: **their**, **house** (page 12)

We can stay at their house.

Writing sentence: **school**, **friend** (page 34)

At school, Jack is my best friend.

Writing sentence: **would**, **magic** (page 34)

Would he ever find the magic lamp?

Writing sentence: **animal**, **dragon** (page 38)

A dragon is a strange animal.

Writing sentence: **garden**, **different** (page 38)

The garden looked different at night.

two- and three-part words page 5	spellings: ur sound page 9	adding ies page 11	adding ed page 18
wagon	burst	tray	pray
motorcycle	thirst	spy	cry
caravan	worm	play	stay
scooter	early	bully	marry
tractor	dirt	penny	annoy
tandem	blur	jockey	tidy
helicopter	kerb	lady	fray
steamroller	hurl	bunny	copy
airship	heard	monkey	display
minibus	worse	puppy	reply
engine	whirl	ferry	
ambulance	search	Monday	

Phase Six Book 2

spellings: or sound page 22	adding y page 23	past tense page 26	adding ful page 28
snort	curl	grow	wish
core	slip	shake	joy
your	slime	slide	shame
laws	snow	sweep	boast
more	nut	sell	faith
floor	taste	throw	forget
gnaw	grump	shook	hate
pour	fog	grew	help
horse	laze	threw	hope
shore	chill	swept	pain
squawk	snap	slid	play
sport	scare	sold	hand

Phase Six Book 2

adding ly page 30	colour words page 34	adding un, dis pages 37–38	adding er, est page 41
kind	amber	lucky	bright
slight	beige	happy	proud
love	bronze	load	kind
smart	grey	fair	mad
fair	crimson	fit	wet
brave	cream	safe	thin
soft	lavender	tidy	tame
wise	maroon	please	fine
even	yellow	like	rude
sudden	lemon	cover	pretty
lone	tangerine	order	silly
swift		own	lucky

Phase Six Book 2

Learning to spell: **colour** (page 8)

> What colour eyes do you have?

Learning to spell: days and months (page 20)

> The date is Tuesday
> 12th December.

Learning to spell: number words (page 33)

> Fourteen girls and sixteen boys makes a class of thirty children.

Learning to spell: colour words (page 34)

> His cloak was scarlet and purple with gold stars on it.

Learning to spell: words for stories (page 36)

> The old woman lived with her daughter in a little tiny cottage.

Introducing proofreading (page 7)

One day Mike and Polly went to sayl their toy boet at the park. But when they reeched the park the gats were locked.

Introducing suffixes **y** (page 23)

Today it was · rainy · and · blowy · .

windy · cloudy · stormy · frosty

foggy · sunny · hazy · icy

Introducing suffixes **ful** (page 28)

Adam is always helpful and cheerful .

hopeful · joyful · playful

useful · thoughtful · careful

From: *Sound Phonics: Teacher's Resource Book* by Carol Matchett (ISBN 978 07217 1224 6). Copyright © Schofield & Sims Ltd, 2014. Published by Schofield & Sims Ltd, Dogley Mill, Fenay Bridge, Huddersfield HD8 0NQ, UK (www.schofieldandsims.co.uk). This page may be photocopied after purchase for use within your school or institution only.

Phase Six Book 2

Introducing suffixes **ly** (page 30)

> The hare ran quickly while the tortoise plodded slowly.

Introducing prefixes **un** and **dis** (page 35)

> The lion was very unhappy.
> He disliked being woken early.
> He was most displeased and whoever woke him might be rather unlucky.

Introducing suffixes **er** and **est** (page 40)

> "I am only small," said the first billy goat.
> "I am even smaller," said the second billy goat.
> "I am the smallest one of all," said the little baby goat.

Date: _____

Key focus of the activity or observation:

Description of activity:

Context:

Name	What does the child do or say?	Achievements and difficulties	Next steps

Assessment resources

Name: _____ Date: _____

Focus	The child can...	Comments
Sound discrimination	<ul><li>identify familiar sounds</li><li>distinguish between sounds</li><li>copy or imitate sounds</li><li>talk about sounds using appropriate vocabulary</li></ul>	
Rhythm	<ul><li>join in with words and actions</li><li>speak the words clearly</li><li>move in time with the beat or rhythm</li><li>change speed and volume of delivery when asked</li></ul>	
Rhyme	<ul><li>recognise when words rhyme</li><li>suggest a word that rhymes with a given word</li><li>distinguish between rhyming and non-rhyming words</li><li>continue a rhyming string</li></ul>	
Alliteration	<ul><li>recognise and respond to alliteration</li><li>suggest an object or name that begins with a given initial sound</li><li>hear and say initial sounds in words</li><li>discriminate between initial sounds</li></ul>	
Oral blending and segmenting	<ul><li>blend spoken sounds into whole word</li><li>segment spoken words into separate sounds.</li></ul>	

Assessment resources

Letter sound check (page 44)

Date:_____

Point to the letters in turn and tick the appropriate box if the child says the correct sound.

Name:					
s					
a					
t					
p					
i					
n					
m					
d					
g					
o					
c					
k					
e					
u					
r					
h					
b					
f					
l					
Letters to revise:					

Assessment resources

Name: _____

Oral blending (page 45)

Date: _____

Say the sounds and ask the child to blend them. Tick if correct, or record any inaccuracies.

	Response
r-a-t	
f-o-g	
n-i-p	
m-e-t	
h-u-g	

Blending for reading (page 45)

Date: _____

The child should sound and blend the words given. Tick if correct, or record any inaccuracies.

	Response: sound talk	**Response: blending**
up		
if		
am		
tan		
din		

Oral segmenting (page 45)

Date: _____

Say the word and ask the child to repeat it in sound talk. Tick if correct, or record any inaccuracies.

	Response
dog	
net	
mug	
tap	

Segmenting for spelling (page 45)

Date: _____

*Ask the child to spell four simple words, such as **am**, **up**, **is** and **on**. Ask the child to say the word in sound talk, and then tell you what letters to write. Tick if correct, or record any inaccuracies.*

	Response: sound talk	**Response: letter choice**

Assessment resources

Sound check (Book 1 page 41; Book 2 page 43)

Date: _____

Point to the graphemes in turn and tick the appropriate box if the child says the correct sound.

Name:					
ff					
ll					
ss					
ck					
j					
v					
w					
x					
y					
z					
qu					
ch					
sh					
th					
ng					

ai					
ee					
igh					
oa					
oo					
ar					
or					
ur					
ow					
oi					
ear					
air					
er					
ure*					
Graphemes to revise:					

** only include **ure** in the assessment if it has been taught*

Name: _____

Blending check (page 42)

Date: _____

Ask the child to sound and blend the words given. Tick if correct, or record any inaccuracies.

	Response: sound talk	Response: word (exactly as said)
yet		
jag		
vat		
tax*		
wax*		
well		
yuck		
quit*		
jazz		
rang		
chill		
shell		
shock		
check		
rung		
thick		

*ks and kw sounds taught for the letters x and q are both actually two phonemes but at this stage children should treat them as one phoneme

Segmenting check (page 43)

Date: _____

Ask the child to sound each word and tell you which letters to write. Tick if correct, or record any inaccuracies.

	Response: sound talk	Response: grapheme choice
net		
bat		
cap		
van		
six		
web		
well		
sack		
bell		
chick		
fish		
king		

Assessment resources

Name: _____

Blending for reading (page 44)   Date: _____

Ask the child to sound and blend the words given. Tick if correct, or record any inaccuracies.

	Response: sound talk	Response: word (exactly as said)
joil		
zear		
yowd		
gair		
thurg		
vight		
waiper		

Segmenting for spelling (page 44)   Date: _____

Ask the child to sound each word and tell you which words to write. Tick if correct, or record any inaccuracies.

	Response: sound talk	Response: grapheme choice
sheep		
jar		
tooth		
coach		
torch		
owl		

Assessment resources

Name: _____

Phase Three Book 1: word check (page 44)　　　　Date: _____

Tick the word if the child reads it automatically.

Name:					
the					
to					
I					
no					
go					
he					
she					
we					
me					
be					
at					
is					
it					
in					
can					
not					
get					
will					
this					
with					
them					

Phase Three Book 2: tricky word check (page 46)　　　　Date: _____

Tick the tricky word if the child reads it automatically.

Name:					
the					
was					
my					
you					
her					
they					
all					
are					

Name: _____

Blending for reading (page 44)   **Date:** _____

Ask the child to sound and blend the given words. Tick if correct, or record any inaccuracies.

	Response: sound talk	Response: word (exactly as said)
selt		
namp		
fent		
plab		
stog		
flim		
thrig		
shrop		
foast		
plort		
breen		
starp		
frist		
crunk		
stunch		

Segmenting for spelling (page 44)   **Date:** _____

Ask the child to say the words in sound talk and write or tell you the letters needed in the phoneme frame. Tick if correct, or record any inaccuracies.

	Response: segmenting	Response: grapheme choice
ant		
tent		
step		
snail		
crust		

*From: **Sound Phonics: Teacher's Resource Book** by Carol Matchett (ISBN 978 07217 1224 6). Copyright © Schofield & Sims Ltd, 2014. Published by Schofield & Sims Ltd, Dogley Mill, Fenay Bridge, Huddersfield HD8 0NQ, UK (www.schofieldandsims.co.uk). This page may be photocopied after purchase for use within your school or institution only.*

Tricky word check (page 46)   Date: _____

Tick the tricky word if the child reads it automatically.

Name:					
said					
so					
do					
have					
like					
some					
come					
were					
there					
little					
one					
when					
what					
out					
all					

*From: **Sound Phonics: Teacher's Resource Book** by Carol Matchett (ISBN 978 07217 1224 6). Copyright © Schofield & Sims Ltd, 2014. Published by Schofield & Sims Ltd, Dogley Mill, Fenay Bridge, Huddersfield HD8 0NQ, UK (www.schofieldandsims.co.uk). This page may be photocopied after purchase for use within your school or institution only.*

Sound check (Book 1 page 43; Book 2 page 44; Book 3 page 43)   **Date:** _____

Point to the graphemes in turn and tick the appropriate box if the child says the correct sound.

Name:					
ay					
ou					
ie					
ea					
oy					
ue					
aw					
ew					
oe					
au					
ir					
ey					
a-e					
e-e					
i-e					
o-e					
u-e					
eer					
are					
wh					
ph					
mb					
kn					
gn					
wr					
tch					
ve					
dge					
Graphemes to revise:					

Name:

Blending for reading (page 44)

Date:

Ask the child to sound and blend the given words. Tick if correct, or record any inaccuracies.

	Response: sound talk	**Response: word (exactly as said)**
raul		
froy		
glout		
blie		
whike*		
proke*		
grawl		
rame*		
breaper		
phinkey		
shirlrue		
shaying		

check that the child recognises the split grapheme and says the long vowel sound in these words

Segmenting for spelling (page 44)

Date:

Ask the child to say the words in sound talk and write the word down. Tick if correct, or record any inaccuracies.

	Response: oral segmenting	**Response: graphemes written**
paw		
spade		
teapot		
tray		
skirt		
wheel		

Assessment resources

Name: _____

Blending for reading (page 45)

Date: _____

Ask the child to sound and blend the given words. Tick if correct, or record any inaccuracies.

	Response: sound talk	Response: blending
parcel		
tidy		
germ		
behind		
ready		
swallow		
reply		
aloud		
danger		
pillow		
ginger		
instead		

Segmenting for spelling (page 45)

Date: _____

Ask the child to say the words in sound talk and write the word down. Tick if correct, or record any inaccuracies.

	Response: oral segmenting	Response: graphemes written
bread		
cage		
fly		
watch		
snowman		
window		

Assessment resources

Name: _____

Blending for reading (page 44)

Date: _____

Ask the child to sound and blend the given words. Tick if correct, or record any inaccuracies.

	Response: sound talk	**Response: blended word**
blind		
swift		
grace		
ginger		
bellow		
spied		
shriek		
ready		
steamer		
mermaid		
spying		
squash		

Segmenting for spelling (page 44)

Date: _____

Ask the child to say the words in sound talk and write the word down. Tick if correct, or record any inaccuracies.

	Response: oral segmenting	**Response: graphemes written**
bridge		
house		
bear		
rainbow		
thirteen		
snowflake		

Assessment resources

Phase Five Book 1: tricky word check (page 46)

Date: _____

Tick the tricky word if the child reads it automatically.

Name:					
oh					
people					
Mr					
Mrs					
their					
looked					
asked					
called					

Phase Five Book 2: tricky word check (page 46)

Date: _____

Name:					
could					
would					
should					
where					
what					
who					
many					
any					
have					
your					

Phase Five Book 3: high-frequency word check (page 45)

Date: _____

Name:					
looked					
called					
asked					
their					
people					
oh					
Mr					
Mrs					

Assessment resources

From: *Sound Phonics: Teacher's Resource Book* by Carol Matchett (ISBN 978 07217 1224 6). Copyright © Schofield & Sims Ltd, 2014. Published by Schofield & Sims Ltd, Dogley Mill, Fenay Bridge, Huddersfield HD8 0NQ, UK (www.schofieldandsims.co.uk). This page may be photocopied after purchase for use within your school or institution only.

Reading aloud assessment (Book 1 page 44; Book 2 page 44)

Name: _____ **Date:** _____

Story: _____

Note in full any errors made by the child when reading. If a word is omitted, record this by writing 'O' or 'omitted'. If you have to tell the child a word, record this as 'T' or 'told'.

If the child gets stuck on a word, prompt him or her to 'have a go' but give no further assistance.

Word printed	Error made	Notes

Comments

Overall confidence, independence, fluency:	Response to and understanding of story:

Assessment resources

Spelling assessment (Book 1 page 45–46; Book 2 page 45–46)

Name: _____ Date: _____

Tick each focus that the child achieved, or record any inaccuracies.

Focus	Notes
Choosing the correct spelling of phonemes *For example, queen, bear.*	
Spelling two-part words *For example, milkshake, bookmark.*	
Adding ed and ing *For example, started, hugged, liking, flopping.*	
Adding s or es *For example, birds, flies, dishes, crashes.*	
Tricky words *For example, water, mouse, different, another.*	
Adding other vowel suffixes *For example, harder, lazier.*	
Adding other consonant suffixes *For example, ful.*	
Adding prefixes *For example, un.*	

Assessment resources

Letter formation

Date: _____

Tick the letter if the child can form it correctly, recording any inaccuracies in the 'Notes' box.

Name:					
a					
b					
c					
d					
e					
f					
g					
h					
i					
j					
k					
l					
m					
n					
o					
p					
q					
r					
s					
t					
u					
v					
w					
x					
y					
z					
Notes:					

Assessment resources

From: **Sound Phonics: Teacher's Resource Book** by Carol Matchett (ISBN 978 07217 1224 6). Copyright © Schofield & Sims Ltd, 2014. Published by Schofield & Sims Ltd, Dogley Mill, Fenay Bridge, Huddersfield HD8 0NQ, UK (www.schofieldandsims.co.uk). This page may be photocopied after purchase for use within your school or institution only.